MENUS AND MEALS FOR THE COST CONSCIOUS COOK

CHEAP
eats

MENUS AND MEALS FOR THE COST CONSCIOUS COOK

CHEAP *eats*

by Joanna Lamiri

LifeStyle

To Mohamed, Sam and Milly,
my three chief recipe tasters!

Photography by Tine Drost

This edition first published in Great Britain in 1999 by
LifeStyle
An imprint of Parkgate Books
Kiln House, 210 New Kings Road, London SW6 4NZ

© 1999 Parkgate Books

A CIP catalogue record for this book is available from the British Library.

ISBN 1-902617-14-2

Printed and bound in Hong Kong

CHEAP*eats*

Gammon Steaks with Parsley Sauce

Grilled Trout with Almonds

Herrings in Oatmeal with Grapefruit Relish

Leek Parcels with Cheese Sauce

Leek & Mushroom Gratin

Mackerel with Gooseberries

Marinated Grilled Chicken

Minced Beef and Pasta Bake

Orange Chicken

Oriental Salmon Steaks

Pasta with Sausages

Pasta with Tomato & Cream Cheese Sauce

Perfect Macaroni Cheese

Perfect Mashed Potatoes

Pork Escalopes with Cheese

Roast Vegetable Medley

Salmon Steaks with Crème Fraîche & Watercress

Spanish Omelette

Spicy Chicken Pasta Sauce

Spicy Lamb with Potatoes

Steak with Blue Cheese Butter

Thai Vegetable Curry

Tofu, Yellow Bean Sauce & Mangetout Stir-fry

Traditional Fish Cakes

Tuna Bake

Turkey with Sage & Grapes

Vegetarian Noodles

Puddings 77

Baked Bananas

Boozy Bread & Butter Pudding

Chocolate Sensation

Classic Chocolate Mousse

Dried Fruit Compôte with Greek Yogurt

Fruit Salad on a Budget

Norwegian Apple Cake

Queen of Puddings

Raspberry Sensation

Rice Pudding with Dried Fruits

Steamed Syrup Pudding

Strawberries Dipped in Chocolate

Zabaglione

Smoothies

Apricot & Orange

Banana & Orange

Apple & Pear

For Menu Suggestions see page 94 and for a Conversion Table see page 96

Shop around

Eating well doesn't have to be a costly business. Of course, if you have a bottomless purse, you can live off caviar, champagne and foie gras. But even on a budget you can enjoy a wide range of imaginative, nutritious and satisfying dishes without relying on cheap convenience foods. There are some cunning ways in which you can keep your food bills down: take advantage of supermarket special offers (buy one, get one free, etc.) and maybe freeze the free item; shop around, and buy fruit, vegetables, spices, herbs and specialist ingredients from street markets and ethnic stores – a huge bunch of coriander will cost about the same as a few sprigs from the supermarket. And, if you have a garden or allotment, why not try growing your own vegetables and herbs? Many are easy to cultivate and will save you a lot of money, especially if you operate a barter system with friends and neighbours!

Healthy eating

Nutritionists have found that the healthiest diets are those that focus on carbohydrates and vegetables, with protein playing a much smaller role. This is good news for those on a budget as it means bulking your meals out with vegetables, rice, potatoes and pasta, and using less meat, poultry and fish. In all my recipes, it is quite possible to decrease the amount of meat given and increase the vegetables and carbohydrates if you wish. You can also substitute beans and pulses for meat and fish in many cases. And serving good, crusty bread with a meal will always make it go further.

Cheap protein

Bear in mind, too, that certain cuts of meat are cheaper. Ask your local butcher or supermarket fresh meat counter for advice. Stewing lamb, for example, is great value for money and, slow-cooked, gives a delicious result. Fish such as mackerel, herrings and trout are good value, while farmed salmon is no longer the luxury it once was.

Store cupboard

One of the problems in following recipes is that they often list an expensive ingredient, such as olive oil, balsamic vinegar and other non-perishable items. My advice is to buy one extra thing each week, whether you need it or not, until you have built up an impressive store cupboard. Ingredients that fall into this category include anchovy fillets, anchovy paste (useful for sauces and casseroles), raspberry vinegar (delicious on steak or in dressings), dried mushrooms, Oriental pastes and condiments and basmati rice.

Dried, frozen or tinned

Although my recipes specify tinned pulses, such as lentils, kidney beans, chickpeas and so on, you can, of course, use dried ones and simply follow the instructions on the packet. Buying frozen ingredients is also a cheaper option than fresh in many cases.

Timings

These will always be approximate, since if you use, for example, a metal dish, the food will cook far quicker than in a china pudding bowl.

Key

Time:
The time it takes to make

Skill ratings:
★ = very, very simple;
★★ very simple; ★★★ simple

Seasonal

One of the most foolproof ways of getting your money's worth is to buy what's in season. Seasonal food tastes better, as well as being cheaper! The following chart identifies what to buy when:

JANUARY/FEBRUARY

Fruit: apples, bananas, clementines, cranberries, grapefruit, grapes, kiwi fruit, lemons, mangoes, oranges, pears, pomegranates, early rhubarb

Vegetables: broccoli, Brussels sprouts, cabbage, carrots, celery, leeks, mushrooms, parsnips, potatoes, swede, sweet potatoes

MARCH/APRIL

Fruit: apples, bananas, grapefruit, grapes, lemons, mangoes, melons, pears, pineapple, rhubarb, tangerines, limes, oranges

Vegetables: asparagus, aubergines, broccoli, Brussels sprouts, cabbage, carrots, cauliflowers, cucumbers, leeks, mushrooms, onions, parsnips, peppers, spring greens, swedes

MAY

Fruit: apples, apricots, avocados, bananas, grapes, kiwi fruit, lemons, limes, mangoes, melons, oranges, pears, strawberries

Vegetables: asparagus, aubergines, beans, broccoli, cauliflowers, courgettes, fennel, leeks, mushrooms, peppers, potatoes, spinach, sweet potatoes

JUNE

Fruit: apricots, avocados, bananas, cherries, grapes, kiwi fruit, lemons, oranges, peaches, plums, strawberries

Vegetables: asparagus, aubergines, beans, broccoli, carrots, cauliflowers, courgettes, fennel, lettuce, mangetout, mushrooms, peas, peppers, potatoes, spinach, spring onions, corn on the cob, sweet potatoes, tomatoes

JULY

Fruit: apricots, avocados, bananas, blackcurrants, blueberries, cherries, gooseberries, grapes, melons, nectarines, peaches, raspberries, redcurrants, strawberries

Vegetables: artichokes, aubergines, beans, broccoli, carrots, cauliflowers, courgettes, cucumbers, lettuce, mushrooms, okra, peppers, spinach, spring onions, tomatoes

AUGUST

Fruit: apples, avocados, bananas, blackberries, blueberries, grapefruit, grapes, gooseberries, kiwi fruit, lemons, melons, nectarines, peaches, pears, raspberries, redcurrants, strawberries

Vegetables: artichokes, aubergines, beans, broccoli, carrots, celery, Chinese leaves, courgettes, fennel, lettuce, mangetout, marrows, mushrooms, onions, peppers, potatoes, spring onions, corn on the cob, tomatoes.

buys

SEPTEMBER

Fruit: avocados, bananas, dates, figs, grapefruit, grapes, kiwi fruit, melons, nectarines, passion fruit, peaches, pears, plums, raspberries, strawberries

Vegetables: artichokes, aubergines, beans, broccoli, cabbage, carrots, cauliflowers, celery, courgettes, fennel, lettuce, mangetout, marrows, mushrooms, onions, parsnips, peppers, potatoes, pumpkin, spring onions, squash, corn on the cob, tomatoes

OCTOBER

Fruit: apples, bananas, coconuts, dates, grapefruit, grapes, lemons, pears, pineapples, plums, pomegranates, satsumas

Vegetables: aubergines, beans, broccoli, Brussels sprouts, cabbage, carrots, cauliflowers, celery, leeks, lettuce, marrows, onions, parsnips, peppers, potatoes, pumpkins, spinach, spring onions, squash, corn on the cob, tomatoes

NOVEMBER

Fruit: apples, bananas, coconuts, cranberries, grapes, kiwi fruit, lemons, mangoes, melons, nuts, oranges, pears, pineapples, pomegranates, satsumas

Vegetables: broccoli, Brussels sprouts, cabbage, carrots, celery, leeks, lettuces, mangetout, mushrooms, okra, onions, parsnips, potatoes, swedes, turnips

DECEMBER

Fruit: apples, avocados, bananas, clementines, coconuts, cranberries, dates, grapefruit, grapes, kiwi fruit, lemons, mangoes, melons, nuts, oranges, pears, pineapple, satsumas

Vegetables: broccoli, Brussels sprouts, cabbage, carrots, celery, cucumbers, leeks, lettuces, mushrooms, onions, parsnips, potatoes, spring onions

Meat is also affected by seasonality, with spring lamb being a good buy, and venison in autumn. Turkey is a good substitute for chicken around Christmas time.

But the essential message of this book is to remember that eating on a budget doesn't mean losing out nutritionally – or aesthetically. With careful shopping and seasonal choices, it is perfectly possible to eat well all year round.

Soups

Chickpea Soup

INGREDIENTS

2 tbsp olive oil

200g (7oz) tube tomato purée

handful of fresh coriander
(see Budget Note)

900ml (1½ pints) water or
chicken stock

2 x 400g (14oz) cans chickpeas

salt and ground black pepper

2 tsp plain flour

1 beaten egg (optional)

lemon wedges and
crusty bread to serve

METHOD

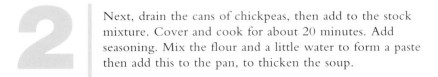

1 Heat the oil in a large pan. Add the tomato purée and the coriander and cook for 2-3 minutes. Stir in a little stock to dilute the mixture, then add the remainder of the stock stirring continuously.

2 Next, drain the cans of chickpeas, then add to the stock mixture. Cover and cook for about 20 minutes. Add seasoning. Mix the flour and a little water to form a paste then add this to the pan, to thicken the soup.

3 Just before serving, stir in the beaten egg and allow to cook for a further 2 minutes to give the soup an attractive marbled appearance. Serve with lemon wedges and crusty bread.

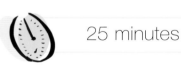 25 minutes

 ★

Serves 4

BUDGET NOTE

Street markets and ethnic food shops are a good, cheap source of fresh herbs, such as coriander, especially if buying large quantities. Store it in the fridge in a plastic bag and it will last for days.

Minted Pea & Lettuce Soup

METHOD

1 In a large pan, melt the butter and cook the shallots for about 10 minutes until soft, but not brown. Add the peas, lettuce and sugar, and cook for a further 10 minutes, stirring from time to time.

2 Slowly add the stock and the mint, reserving a few leaves for garnishing. Stir continuously and bring to the boil. Turn down the heat and allow the soup to simmer for a further 10 minutes. Season well.

3 Transfer the soup to a blender and blend to the required thickness, this is purely a matter of individual taste. To serve, add a swirl of crème fraîche to each serving and garnish with mint leaves.

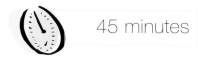 45 minutes

 ★ ★ ★

Serves 4

INGREDIENTS

55g (2oz) butter

110g (4oz) shallots, finely chopped

450g (1lb) pack frozen peas

1 lettuce heart, sliced

2 tbsp caster sugar

1.2 litres (2 pints) vegetable or chicken stock

a handful of fresh mint leaves

salt and ground black pepper

crème fraîche to serve (optional)

Spicy Lentil Soup

INGREDIENTS

2 tbsp oil

1 large onion, finely chopped

1 clove garlic, crushed

1 tbsp ground cumin

1 tsp chilli powder

2 x 400g (14oz) cans green lentils, drained

900ml (1½ pints) vegetable or chicken stock

salt and ground black pepper

METHOD

1 Heat the oil in a large pan over a medium heat, then add the onion and garlic. Take care that the oil is not too hot otherwise the ingredients will cook too quickly and burn. Cook for about 10 minutes until soft, then add the spices.

2 Stir the soup well and cook over a medium heat for a further 2-3 minutes. Drain the cans of green lentils, add them to the soup and cook, stirring, for a further 5 minutes.

3 Add the vegetable or chicken stock slowly, stirring continuously, and bring the soup to the boil. Turn down the heat and allow to simmer for approximately 20 minutes. Finally, season with salt and pepper to taste and serve.

 45 minutes

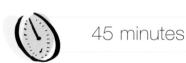 ★ ★

Serves 4

Three-Bean Soup

METHOD

1 Heat the oil over a medium heat, then add the onion and garlic. Cook for about 10 minutes until soft, but not browned. Add the tomatoes, celery, carrots, thyme and stock. Stir well, cover and allow to simmer for about 20 minutes.

2 While the vegetable and stock mixture is simmering, drain the canned kidney beans, cannellini beans and chickpeas well, then rinse with cold water to remove the canning liquid.

3 Add the kidney beans, cannellini beans and chickpeas to the soup and cook for a further 5-10 minutes until the beans are hot through. Stir in the parsley, season with salt and pepper and serve hot.

 50 minutes

  ★

Serves 4

INGREDIENTS

2 tbsp olive oil

1 large onion, finely chopped

2 cloves garlic, crushed

1 x 400g (14oz) can chopped tomatoes

2 sticks celery, finely chopped

2 carrots, finely chopped

1 tsp dried thyme

900ml (1½ pints) vegetable or chicken stock

1 x 400g (14oz) can kidney beans

1 x 400g (14oz) can cannellini beans

1 x 400g (14oz) can chickpeas

1 tbsp chopped flat-leaf parsley

salt and ground black pepper

Salads

Bean & Lentil Salad

INGREDIENTS

2 x 400g (14oz) cans beans,
eg cannellini, haricot or
black eye beans

1 x 400g (14oz) can green lentils

1 tbsp oil

1 large onion, finely chopped

1 clove garlic, crushed

110g (4oz) bacon, chopped

DRESSING

3 tbsp olive oil

1 tbsp balsamic vinegar or ½ tbsp
red wine vinegar

1 tbsp finely chopped flat-leaf
parsley

METHOD

1 Drain the canned beans and lentils, then rinse well with cold water to remove the canning liquid. Heat the oil, then cook the onion and garlic for about 5 minutes, until soft but not browned.

2 Add the bacon and cook for a further 5 minutes until the bacon is cooked. Meanwhile, in a small bowl, combine the oil, vinegar and parsley for the dressing, and stir well.

3 Add the beans and lentils to the pan and heat thoroughly. Once cooked, remove from the pan and place the salad on a serving plate. Pour the dressing over and serve warm with crusty bread.

 25 minutes

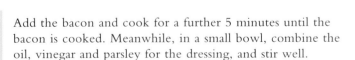 ★ ★

Serves 4

Broad Bean & Bacon Salad

M E T H O D

1 Dry-fry the chopped streaky bacon until crisp, and set to one side. Heat 1 tbsp oil in a frying pan, then add the onion and garlic. Fry until soft but not browned.

2 Meanwhile, cook the broad beans, then add to the garlic and onion mixture. Add the cooked, reserved bacon and chopped parsley to the mixture and cook for about 5 minutes until hot.

3 Mix in the remaining oil and lemon juice and season well with salt and ground black pepper. This salad can be served either warm or cold with salad leaves and crusty bread.

 25 minutes

 ★

Serves 4

I N G R E D I E N T S

230g (8oz) streaky bacon, chopped

3 tbsp olive oil

1 onion, finely chopped

1 clove garlic, crushed

450g (1lb) fresh or frozen broad beans

2 tbsp chopped flat-leaf parsley

1 tbsp lemon juice

salt and ground black pepper

salad leaves and crusty bread to serve

Chicken, Blue Cheese & Apple Salad

INGREDIENTS

230g (8oz) cooked chicken breast

2 crisp eating apples

3 tbsp chopped walnuts

230g (8oz) blue cheese, eg Stilton

mixed salad leaves

DRESSING

3 tbsp sunflower oil

1 tbsp apple juice

2 tsp honey

salt and ground black pepper

METHOD

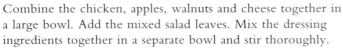

1 Chop the cooked chicken into bite-size pieces. Core and slice the apples into wedges, and then in half again, chop the nuts finely and cut the cheese into cubes.

2 Combine the chicken, apples, walnuts and cheese together in a large bowl. Add the mixed salad leaves. Mix the dressing ingredients together in a separate bowl and stir thoroughly.

3 Add the dressing mixture to the salad ingredients, toss and serve immediately. This salad should be eaten immediately, otherwise the apple pieces will turn brown.

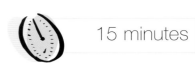 15 minutes

 ★

Serves 4

TIP BOX

This salad can either be served warm or cold, and can be made with fresh chicken, but is also a good recipe for any leftovers from a roast.

Grilled Pepper & Tomato Salad

METHOD

1 Halve the peppers and place, skin side up, on a grill pan. Cook under a hot grill for about 20-25 minutes or until the skins have blackened. Seal the peppers in a plastic bag and leave to cool for about 10 minutes – this will make them much easier to peel.

2 While the peppers are cooling, put the tomatoes on a sheet of foil under the grill for about 10 minutes until blackened, then remove the skins. Once the peppers have cooled, remove the stalks, seeds and skin and cut roughly into quarters.

3 Mix the peppers, tomatoes and garlic. Season well then stir in the olive oil. Chill until ready to serve. The salad can be served with either tuna and hard boiled eggs or alternatively grilled meat or fish.

40 minutes

★ ★

Serves 8

INGREDIENTS

4 medium red peppers

2 medium green peppers

620g (1lb 6oz) ripe tomatoes, halved

4-5 cloves garlic, peeled and crushed

salt and ground black pepper

2 tbsp olive oil

canned tuna and hard-boiled eggs to serve

Mushroom & Salami Salad

INGREDIENTS

3 tbsp olive oil

1 tbsp lemon juice

salt and ground black pepper

170g (6oz) mushrooms, sliced

110g (4oz) salami, chopped

salad leaves

salt and ground black pepper

METHOD

1 Mix the olive oil and lemon juice together, stirring well. Next, either wipe the mushrooms with a cloth to clean them or peel them. Slice, or chop the mushrooms.

2 You can use any type of salami for this recipe – or substitute this with ham. Chop the salami and mix with the mushrooms. Next pour the oil and lemon juice mixture over the salami and mushrooms.

3 Stir the ingredients well, season and leave in a cool place for about 1 hour to allow the flavours to mingle. Serve on a bed of mixed salad leaves with salt and ground black pepper.

 60 minutes

 ★

Serves 2

Prawn & Couscous Salad

METHOD

1 Cook the couscous according to the packet instructions. Meanwhile, chop the cucumber, tomatoes and spring onions. Grate the lemon rind using the finest section of your grater, then squeeze the juice into a cup and leave to one side.

2 If you are using fresh prawns, ensure that the heads, tails and shells are completely removed and rinse well with water. Shake off any excess water. If you are using frozen prawns, ensure that they are fully defrosted.

3 Stir the prawns, cucumber, tomatoes and spring onions into the cooked couscous. Add seasoning and the lemon rind and juice to taste.

 20 minutes

 ★ ★

Serves 4

TIP BOX

Couscous originates from Tunisia, where it is considered the national dish, but it is now possible to buy it in every major supermarket (generally you will find it near the rice and pasta).

INGREDIENTS

230g (8oz) medium-grain couscous

half a cucumber, chopped

2 large ripe tomatoes, chopped

4 spring onions, finely chopped

1 large lemon

230g (8oz) shelled, cooked prawns

salt and ground black pepper

flat-leaf parsley to garnish

Sausage & Soured Cream Salad

INGREDIENTS

230g (8oz) pork sausages

55g (2oz) onion

140ml (5fl oz) carton soured cream

salt and ground black pepper

pinch of cayenne pepper

crusty bread and salad
leaves to serve

METHOD

1 Cook the sausages, allow them to cool for a few minutes and then cut into bite-size pieces. Peel the onion and cut into rings. As an alternative, you may wish to use a red onion as these are slightly milder in taste when eaten raw.

2 Combine the sausage pieces and onion rings and slowly mix in the soured cream. Start with half of the carton, then add bit by bit to the mixture until the sausages are evenly coated.

3 Season the sausage and soured cream mixture with salt and pepper and a pinch of cayenne pepper. Serve on a bed of salad leaves with crusty bread.

 15 minutes

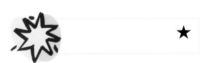 ★

Serves 2

TIP BOX

Salads are often tastiest when few ingredients are used, as here. This recipe can be adapted or added to, to suit your own tastes. We have suggested pork sausages, but any type of sausage can be used.

Smoked Mackerel & Horseradish Salad

METHOD

1 Using a fork, flake the smoked mackerel, discarding the skin. Finely chop the spring onion. Mix the mackerel and spring onion and place on a bed of shredded lettuce. It is always preferable to tear lettuce with your hands, as cutting with a knife will bruise the leaves and cause them to brown.

2 Mix about 2 tsp horseradish sauce, or more if you prefer a hotter taste, into the carton of crème fraîche. Pour this over the salad.

3 Squeeze the lemon juice over the salad, season generously with salt and ground black pepper, then garnish with flat-leaf parsley to serve.

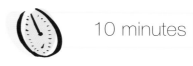 10 minutes

  ★

Serves 2

INGREDIENTS

230g (8oz) smoked mackerel

1 spring onion, finely chopped

crisp shredded lettuce or mixed salad leaves to serve

horseradish sauce

200g (7oz) carton crème fraîche

the juice of ½ a lemon

salt and ground black pepper

flat leaf parsley to garnish

Thai-Style Seafood Salad

INGREDIENTS

2 x 290g (10oz) jars prepared seafood in oil (available from supermarkets)

½ red pepper, sliced

1 small red chilli, finely chopped

2 limes

1 clove garlic, crushed

3 kaffir lime leaves

1 stalk lemon grass

salt and ground black pepper

salad leaves to serve

lemon wedges to garnish (optional)

METHOD

1 Drain the seafood, reserving the oil. Slice the pepper and finely chop the red chilli (ensure that you wash your hands thoroughly after touching the chilli). Grate the rind of the limes, then halve them and squeeze the juice into a small bowl.

2 Heat the oil, reserved from the jars of seafood, then add the garlic, lime leaves, sliced pepper, chilli, lemon grass, lime juice and lime rind and cook for about 2-3 minutes. Remove from the heat and pour over the seafood while still warm. Season generously with salt and ground black pepper.

3 Leave in a cool place to marinate for about 1 hour. Serve on a bed of salad leaves and garnish with lemon wedges.

 70 minutes

  ★ ★

Serves 4

Snacks

Breakfast Hash

INGREDIENTS

2 tbsp oil

8 sausages, cut into two
or three pieces, depending on size

1 x 400g (14oz) can
chopped tomatoes

2 red or green peppers, sliced

6 eggs

salt and ground black pepper

crusty bread to serve

METHOD

1 Heat the oil in a large frying pan, then cook the sausages until browned. Add the chopped tomatoes, bring to the boil then simmer for 20 minutes over a medium heat until the tomato sauce has reduced.

2 Slice the peppers and add to the pan. Next add the eggs, cracking each into the pan. Cook for a further 5 minutes, gently basting the eggs with the tomato sauce until they are lightly cooked.

3 Finish off under a hot grill for about 5 minutes, or until the eggs are set. Season well with salt and ground black pepper and serve piping hot with crusty bread.

 30 minutes

  ★ ★

Serves 6

Chicken Liver Paté

METHOD

1 Melt 30g (1oz) butter in a pan and fry the chicken livers over a medium heat for about 5 minutes, stirring continuously. Using a slotted spoon, transfer them to a blender or press through a sieve.

2 Melt a further 110g (4oz) butter and add to the mixture. Add the remaining ingredients, season and blend until smooth. Transfer to a serving dish and pat the mixture down well. Melt the remaining butter and pour over the paté.

3 When the paté has cooled, cover and chill for up to 2 days. Serve with hot crusty bread or toast, salad leaves and chutney.

15 minutes

★ ★ ★

Serves 4

INGREDIENTS

200g (7oz) butter

230g (8oz) chicken livers

1 tsp mustard powder

½ tsp ground mace

1 tsp fresh chopped thyme or
¼ tsp dried thyme

1 clove garlic, crushed

salt and ground black pepper

hot crusty bread or toast, salad
leaves and chutney to serve

Cornbread

INGREDIENTS

230g (8oz) cornmeal or polenta

170g (6oz) plain flour

110g (4oz) caster sugar

3 tsp baking powder

1 egg

300ml (½ pint) milk

30g (1oz) butter,
plus extra for greasing

METHOD

1 Preheat the oven to 200°C (400°F) or Gas Mark 7. Mix the cornmeal or polenta, plain flour, caster sugar and baking powder together in a large bowl.

2 Beat the egg into the milk and melt the butter. Add the melted butter to the egg and milk mixture and stir gently into the dry ingredients until all the ingredients are thoroughly combined.

3 Grease a 20cm (8in) baking tin and pour in the mixture. Transfer to the oven and cook for about 20 minutes or until risen and golden brown. Remove from oven and allow to cool on a wire rack. Serve warm or cold.

30 minutes

★ ★

Serves 8

TIP BOX

This typical American dish is delicious with spicy dishes such as chilli con carne or vegetable curry.

Jacket Potatoes with Curried Chicken or Spicy Ratatouille

METHOD

1 Wash the potato thoroughly. Rub a little oil over the surface of the potato, sprinkle with salt and cook for 1½ –2 hours at 190°C (375°F) or Gas Mark 5.

2 For the curried chicken version: stir the curry paste into the mayonnaise. Chop the chicken into bite-size pieces and stir in the mayonnaise (add extra curry paste to taste).

3 Add the chilli powder to the ratatouille and heat through for a spicy vegetarian option. Fill the potatoes and garnish with flat-leaf parsley to serve.

2 hours

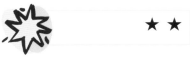
★ ★

Serves 2

INGREDIENTS

1 large potato

cooking oil

salt

2 tsp Indian curry paste

140ml (5fl oz) mayonnaise

230g (8oz) cooked chicken

---

1 large potato

cooking oil

salt

1 tsp chilli powder

425g (15oz) can ratatouille

flat-leaf parsley to garnish

Jacket Potatoes with Salmon or Pesto and Crème Fraîche

INGREDIENTS

1 large potato

cooking oil

salt

juice of ½ lemon

200g (7oz) can of red salmon

salt and ground black pepper

200 ml (7fl oz) carton of
crème fraîche

½ crunchy apple

---

or for pesto and crème fraîche...

2 tbsp of red or green pesto

200 ml (7fl oz) carton of
crème fraîche

salad leaves to garnish

METHOD

1 Wash the potato thoroughly. Rub a little oil over the surface of the potato, sprinkle with salt and cook for 1½ -2 hours at 190°C (375°F) or Gas Mark 5.

 2 hours

  ★ ★

2 Add the juice from the lemon to the drained can of red salmon and season with ground black pepper and salt. Serve with a dash of crème fraîche and garnish with the apple slices.

Serves 2

3 For a tasty vegetarian option, prepare the potato as in step1. Stir the pesto into the carton of crème fraîche, and serve with a garnish of salad leaves.

Pitta Pockets with Tuna

M E T H O D

1 Under a low grill, or in the toaster, lightly toast the pitta breads (this will make them easier to open). Remove from the grill and, with a sharp knife, split each one open to form a pocket.

2 Drain the canned tuna. Slice the tomatoes, cut the cucumber into chunks and shred the lettuce. In a bowl, mix all the ingredients until well combined and season generously with salt and ground black pepper.

3 Place all of the ingredients inside the pitta pockets and top with a dollop of mayonnaise. If you prefer, you could use cooked chicken instead of canned tuna.

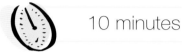 10 minutes

 ★

Serves 2

I N G R E D I E N T S

4 pitta breads

1 x 200g (7oz) tuna

4 tomatoes

half a cucumber

half a crisp
lettuce (eg Iceberg)

mayonnaise to serve

salad leaves to garnish

salt and ground black pepper

Poached Eggs with Hollandaise Sauce

INGREDIENTS

a dash of vinegar

4 large eggs

butter

2 muffins

1 x carton fresh Hollandaise sauce
(available from supermarkets)

a few parsley sprigs to garnish

salt and ground black pepper

METHOD

1 Heat water to a depth of 5cm (2in) in a small saucepan, until the bubbles are barely breaking the surface (any stronger and the eggs will disintegrate). Add a dash of vinegar to the water.

2 Carefully crack the eggs into the pan and cook for between 3-5 minutes, depending on how runny you like them. Spoon water over the eggs towards the end of the cooking time to ensure they are cooked.

3 Using a slotted spoon, remove the eggs from the water and place each one on half a buttered toasted muffin. Spoon over the Hollandaise sauce, garnish with parsley and season with salt and ground black pepper to serve.

 10 minutes

 ★ ★ ★

 Serves 4

Sandwiches

Pear, Blue Cheese & Watercress Serves 2

INGREDIENTS

1 large, ripe pear

110g (4oz) blue cheese, eg Stilton

55g (2oz) watercress

4 large slices bread, buttered

METHOD

1 Fruit and cheese complement each other particularly well in a sandwich as the sweetness of the fruit enhances the flavour of the cheese. You can also try different types of bread.

2 Peel, core and slice the pear. Crumble the cheese and rinse the watercress. Layer the ingredients between the buttered bread to form a sandwich and eat immediately.

3 Other successful fruit and cheese combinations are: apple and cheddar; black grapes and brie; cranberry and camembert. You can add salad leaves and extra fruit to garnish, if you wish.

Sandwiches

Chicken & Mango Chutney Serves 2

METHOD

Place the shredded lettuce on the bread and top with the chicken. Spoon the mango chutney on top and eat immediately.

INGREDIENTS

crisp lettuce, eg Iceberg

4 large slices bread, buttered

110g (4oz) cooked chicken

2 tbsp mango chutney

Roast Beef & Horseradish Serves 2

METHOD

Top the bread with the beef, spread with horseradish to taste and top with the tomatoes. Eat immediately.

INGREDIENTS

4 large slices bread, buttered

2 slices roast beef

2 tsp horseradish sauce

55g (2oz) cherry tomatoes, halved

Scrambled Eggs with Salmon or Bacon

INGREDIENTS

2 rashers of streaky bacon or
30g (1oz) smoked salmon
(see Budget Note)

4 eggs, beaten

55g (2oz) butter

fresh dill sprigs to garnish

salt and ground black pepper

toast or muffins to serve

METHOD

1 If using bacon, cook it until crisp and then cut into small pieces. Beat the eggs together briskly. Heat half the butter in a heavy-based pan. When the butter has melted, add the eggs, stirring continuously so they do not stick.

2 After a minute or so, add the remaining butter and stir until the eggs have scrambled, but are still quite runny. Season with a pinch of salt and ground black pepper (bacon and salmon are both salty so you need not add salt if preferred).

3 Stir the bacon or chopped smoked salmon into the eggs and pile them high on buttered toast or muffins to serve. Garnish with fresh dill sprigs

 10 minutes

 ★ ★

Serves 2

BUDGET NOTE

Look out for smoked salmon trimmings in your local supermarket as these are cheaper and ideal for cooking.

Main

1
2
3

Courses

Baked Cod in a Herb & Cheese Crust

INGREDIENTS

6 cod steaks

oil for brushing

salt and ground black pepper

230g (8oz) breadcrumbs

110g (4oz) mature cheese

2 tbsp flat-leaf parsley, finely chopped

3 tbsp oil

3 lemons and crisp green salad leaves to serve

METHOD

1 Preheat the oven to 200°C (400°F) or Gas Mark 6. Place the cod steaks in a baking tray and brush each one with oil. Season generously with salt and ground black pepper.

2 Mix together the breadcrumbs, cheese, parsley, and oil until thoroughly combined, season, and top each cod steak with the mixture.

3 Cook in the oven for about 15-20 minutes, or until the fish is opaque. Serve with lemon wedges and a crisp salad or new potatoes.

 20 minutes

 ★ ★

Serves 6

Beef, Red Pepper & Beansprout Stir-fry

METHOD

1 Heat the sunflower oil in a wok or large frying pan until very hot, then carefully add the sliced onion. Stir with a wooden spoon for about 3 minutes, until soft, then add the steak strips and cook for a further 5 minutes.

2 Meanwhile, cook the noodles, following the instructions on the packet. Add the peppers and beansprouts to the wok or frying pan, and stir-fry for a further 3 minutes until the vegetables are cooked.

3 Stir in the rice wine, add salt and black pepper to taste and heat through to serve. Place the cooked, drained noodles on a plate and top with the stir-fry.

 15 minutes

  ★ ★

Serves 4

INGREDIENTS

1 tbsp sunflower oil

1 large onion, sliced

340g (12oz) steak, cut into thin strips

2 red peppers, thinly sliced

110g (4oz) beansprouts

2 tbsp rice wine

noodles to serve

Beth's Chilli con Carne

INGREDIENTS

1kg (2lb 2oz) minced beef

2 tbsp oil

3 large onions, sliced

3 cloves garlic, crushed

2 x 400g (14oz) cans chopped tomatoes

2 tbsp chilli powder

1 tbsp ground cumin

1 tsp paprika

salt and ground black pepper

2 x 400g (14oz) cans red kidney beans

soured cream and grated cheese to serve, or cornbread (optional)

METHOD

1 Brown the mince without oil in a large heavy-based casserole or pan, and then put to one side in a bowl. Heat the oil and cook the onions and garlic for about 10 minutes or until soft but not browned.

2 Return the mince to the pan, add the chopped tomatoes, chilli powder, cumin and paprika, then season with salt and freshly ground black pepper. Stir well and bring to the boil, reduce the heat and allow to simmer for 2 hours.

3 Adjust the seasoning if necessary, add the drained kidney beans, then cook for a further 20 minutes. Serve with soured cream and grated cheese or cornbread. (See recipe on page 30)

2½ hours

★ ★

Serves 6-8

Chicken Breasts stuffed with Boursin

METHOD

1 Preheat oven to 190°C (375°F) or Gas Mark 5. With a sharp knife, cut a slit into each chicken breast to make a pocket. Using a teaspoon, fill each pocket with 2-3 tsp Boursin.

2 Close the pocket and secure either with fine string or by pushing a cocktail stick horizontally through the chicken. Brush with oil and season well with salt and ground black pepper.

3 Place the chicken breasts on a baking tray and cook for about 30 minutes, or until cooked through and browned. Remove and serve with a crisp green salad or seasonal vegetables.

 40 minutes

  ★ ★

Serves 4

INGREDIENTS

4 chicken breasts

1 carton Boursin cheese

oil for brushing

salt and ground black pepper

crisp green salad to serve

Chicken, Pak Choi & Bamboo Shoot Stir-fry

INGREDIENTS

1tbsp sunflower oil

1 large onion, finely sliced

1 x 230g (8oz) can bamboo shoots, drained

1 x 230g (8oz) can water chestnuts, drained

170g (6oz) pak choi

340g (12oz) chicken breast

2 tbsp soy sauce

salt and ground black pepper

boiled noodles or rice to serve

flat-leaf parsley to garnish

METHOD

1 Heat the sunflower oil in a wok or large frying pan, then add the finely sliced onion. Cook for about 3 minutes, stirring continuously until soft but not browned. Drain the bamboo shoots and water chestnuts.

2 Wash, trim and chop the pak choi. Cut the chicken breasts into thin strips. Add the chicken and pak choi to the wok and cook for a further 5 minutes, or until the chicken is cooked through, stirring continuously.

3 Add the drained bamboo shoots and water chestnuts and soy sauce, then stir until heated through. Add a small amount of salt (you may not need much due to the soy sauce) and pepper to taste and serve with either noodles or rice.

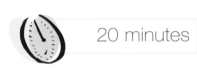 20 minutes

 ★ ★

Serves 4

Classic Lamb Stew

METHOD

1 In a heavy-based pan, heat 2 tbsp oil. Cut the lamb into chunks and add to the pan, in batches. As each batch browns, remove from the pan and put to one side, keeping it warm. do not add too much to the pan at once or it will not brown.

2 Using the juices from the pan, cook the onion and carrots for 10 minutes until soft. You may need to add another tbsp oil. Once the vegetables are soft, return the lamb to the pan. Stir in the tomato purée and flour and cook for 1 minute.

3 Pour in the stock and the Worcestershire sauce. Season with salt and pepper, reduce the heat, cover and simmer for about 1 hour. Finally, add the chickpeas or frozen peas and cook for a further 10 minutes. Serve with crusty bread.

1½ hours

★ ★ ★

Serves 6

INGREDIENTS

oil

1¼kg (3lb) stewing lamb

2 large onions, sliced

230g (8oz) carrots, sliced on the diagonal

2 tsp tomato purée

1 tbsp plain flour

600ml (1 pint) lamb or beef stock

1 tbsp Worcestershire sauce

salt and ground black pepper

1 x 400g (14oz) can chickpeas or 110g (4oz) frozen peas

crusty bread to serve

Cod with Lentils

INGREDIENTS

6 medium cod steaks or 900g (2lb) cod fillet

melted butter

salt and ground black pepper

6 bay leaves

2 tbsp oil

1 large onion, finely chopped

2-3 cloves garlic, crushed

3 tbsp finely chopped parsley

2 x 400g (14oz) cans green lentils, drained

3 lemons

METHOD

1 If using cod fillet, cut it into six even pieces. Place each piece of cod on a piece of baking foil, brush with melted butter, season and add a bay leaf. Fold the foil so that it is airtight, but leave enough space between the top side of the fish and the foil for steam to circulate.

2 Place the foil parcels on a baking tray and cook in a preheated oven at 200°C (400°F) or Gas Mark 6 for about 15 minutes. Meanwhile, heat the oil in a large frying pan. Add the onion, garlic and parsley and cook for about 10 minutes until soft.

3 Add the lentils and continue to cook for about 5 minutes until hot through. Remove the cod from the foil parcels, taking care with the release of steam. Serve the cooked cod on a bed of lentils, with lemon wedges.

 35 minutes

  ★ ★

Serves 6

Easy Paella

METHOD

1 Heat half the oil in a large, heavy-based pan. Chop the onion and pepper and add to the pan with the garlic. Cook for 5-10 minutes, until soft but not browned. Remove the vegetables from the pan and keep warm.

2 Heat the remaining oil, then add the rice and turmeric. Stir for 2-3 minutes until the rice turns opaque, then add the stock. Bring to the boil, cover the pan and simmer until the rice has absorbed all the stock, adding more if necessary.

3 Return the vegetables to the pan, then add the mixed seafood, cooked chicken, chorizo sausage and frozen peas. Heat through for a further 5-10 minutes, then serve.

50 minutes

★ ★

Serves 6

INGREDIENTS

2 tbsp oil

1 medium onion, finely chopped

1 red pepper

2 cloves garlic, crushed

340g (12oz) long-grain rice

1 tsp ground turmeric

600ml (1 pint) chicken stock

1 x 290g (10oz) jar prepared mixed antipasti seafood (from supermarkets)

230g (8oz) cooked chicken

140g (5oz) chorizo sausage (optional)

110g (4oz) frozen peas

Fish Kebabs

INGREDIENTS

230g (8oz) cod fillet,
cut into cubes

230g (8oz) smoked haddock fillet,
cut into cubes

230g (8oz) salmon fillet,
cut into cubes

170g (6oz) cherry tomatoes

juice and rind of 2 lemons,
plus extra to serve

2 tbsp finely chopped flat-leaf
parsley

3 tbsp oil

salt and ground black pepper

salad leaves to serve

METHOD

1 Allow 2 kebabs per person. Cut the cod, haddock and salmon into cubes of roughly the same size. Thread the fish on to eight wooden skewers, alternating with the cherry tomatoes.

2 Grate the lemon rind using a zester or the finest section of your grater. Then halve the lemons and squeeze the juice into a small bowl. Chop the parsley finely. A quick tip here is to put the parsley in a beaker and use scissors to cut it. Mix the oil, lemon zest, juice, parsley, salt and pepper together then brush on to the fish skewers.

3 Place under a hot grill, or even on a barbecue for 5-10 minutes until cooked through, then serve with mixed salad leaves and ground black pepper.

 20 minutes

 ★ ★

Serves 4

Gammon Steaks with Parsley Sauce

METHOD

1 Grill the gammon steaks under a medium grill. In the meantime, put the milk in a pan with the sliced onion, bay leaf and peppercorns. Bring to the boil and remove from the heat. Allow to stand for 10 minutes.

2 Melt about 20g (¾oz)of butter, add the flour and cook, stirring continuously, for 1 minute. Remove from the heat and strain in the hot milk, whisking as you do so to remove any lumps.

3 Bring to the boil, stirring until the sauce thickens. Chop the parsley, reserving a sprig for garnish. Add the chopped parsley, remaining butter and season with salt and pepper Serve the sauce either on top or to the side of the gammon.

30 minutes

  ★ ★

Serves 4

INGREDIENTS

4 gammon steaks

300ml (½pint) milk

1 sliced onion

1 bay leaf

4 black peppercorns

20g (¾oz butter)

1½ tbsp plain flour

55g (2oz) chopped flat-leaf parsley

30g (1oz) butter

salt and ground black pepper

Grilled Trout with Almonds

INGREDIENTS

4 fresh trout

110g (4oz) melted butter

2 lemons

several sprigs parsley

4 tbsp vermouth

110g (4oz) flaked almonds

METHOD

1 Clean and gut the trout. If you are unsure of how to do this, ask your fishmonger to do it for you (most fresh fish bought at supermarkets is already prepared and ready to cook).

2 Melt the butter over a medium heat. Halve the lemons, squeeze the juice into a small bowl and chop the parsley. Brush each trout with melted butter and top with parsley, some lemon juice, 1 tbsp of vermouth and 30g (1oz) of flaked almonds.

3 Grill the trout under a medium grill for 10-15 minutes until cooked through. Spoon the juices from the grill pan over the fish and serve at once with seasonal vegetables or mixed salad leaves.

 20 minutes

 ★ ★

Serves 4

Herrings in Oatmeal with Grapefruit Relish

M E T H O D

1 Season the oatmeal generously with salt and pepper, then roll the herrings in it until well coated. Heat 2 tbsp oil in a large frying pan and, when hot, carefully add the herrings, taking care not to dislodge the oatmeal.

2 Cook for 5-7 minutes on each side until browned and cooked through. While the herrings are cooking, drain the grapefruit if canned, or remove peel and pith if fresh. Chop the grapefruit into bite-size pieces.

3 Using a zester or the finest section of your grater, grate the lemon rind, then halve the lemon and squeeze the juice into a cup. Mix the lemon juice and rind with the grapefruit segments and serve with the grilled herrings.

 15 minutes

  ★ ★

Serves 4

I N G R E D I E N T S

salt and ground black pepper

230g (8oz) oatmeal

8 herrings, gutted and rinsed

oil for frying

1 x 530g (1lb 3oz) can grapefruit segments, or 2 fresh grapefruit

1 lemon

Leek Parcels with Cheese Sauce

INGREDIENTS

6 large leeks, trimmed and washed

salt and ground black pepper

12 slices ham

40g (1½oz) butter

30g (1oz) plain flour

300ml (½ pint) milk

110g (4oz) grated cheese

pinch of nutmeg

extra cheese for sprinkling

warm crusty bread or a crisp green
salad to serve

METHOD

1 Cook the leeks, whole, for about 10 minutes in boiling, salted water until tender, but not too soft, then drain. Meanwhile, make the cheese sauce by melting the butter in a heavy-based pan. Add the flour and stir for 1 minute to make a paste.

2 Gradually add the milk, stirring continuously. When the sauce has thickened, stir in the grated cheese and add a pinch of nutmeg. Season to taste. When the leeks are cool enough to handle, wrap 2 slices of ham round each one and place them tightly in a heatproof dish.

3 Pour the cheese sauce over and sprinkle with extra cheese. Place under a hot grill for a few minutes until the cheese is bubbling and browned. Serve with warm crusty bread or a crisp green salad.

 15 minutes

  ★ ★ ★

Serves 6

Leek & Mushroom Gratin

METHOD

1 Preheat the oven to 200°C (400°F) or Gas Mark 6. Heat half the oil in a pan, then fry the vegetables until lightly browned. Add the stock, chopped parsley and lemon juice and cook, uncovered for about 10 minutes.

2 Transfer the vegetables to a lightly greased ovenproof dish. Sprinkle half the cheese over the vegetables in the dish. Boil the remaining stock and parsley until reduced to half of the amount. Mix the reduced stock with the milk and season to taste. Pour over the vegetables.

3 Mix the remaining cheese with the bread crumbs, remaining oil and salt and ground black pepper then sprinkle over the dish. Cook for about 20 minutes until the topping is golden brown.

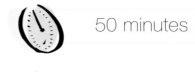

50 minutes

★ ★

Serves 4

INGREDIENTS

1 tbsp oil

450g (1lb) leeks, trimmed and sliced

110g (4oz) mushrooms, wiped and sliced

300ml (½ pint) vegetable stock

2 tbsp chopped flat-leaf parsley

juice of 1 lemon

110g (4oz) Cheddar cheese, grated

140ml (¼ pint) milk

salt and ground black pepper

85g (3oz) fresh breadcrumbs

Mackerel with Gooseberries

INGREDIENTS

4 mackerel, gutted and rinsed

salt and ground black pepper

1 tbsp sunflower oil

340g (12oz) canned or frozen gooseberries

juice of half a lemon

METHOD

1 Season the fish on both sides with salt and ground black pepper. Heat the sunflower oil in a large frying pan, then cook the mackerel for 5-7 minutes on each side until cooked through. Be careful of the hot fat splashing.

2 Meanwhile, drain the gooseberries if canned in syrup, and place in a pan with 5fl oz (¼ pint) water. If the gooseberries are canned in natural juices, however, use this instead of the water.

3 Cook the gooseberries over a low heat with the lemon juice until heated through and very soft. Serve with the cooked mackerel.

 20 minutes

 ★ ★

Serves 4

Marinated Grilled Chicken

METHOD

1 Preheat the oven to 190°C (375°F) or Gas Mark 5. Using a zester or fine grater, grate the rind of the lime, then halve it and squeeze the juice into a bowl or glass. Add the lime rind, garlic, oil and soy sauce. Slice the ginger and add.

2 Add the chicken breasts, turn to coat them well in the marinade, then season and marinate in a cool place for at least 3 hours, preferably overnight.

3 Transfer the chicken to a baking tray, pour the remaining marinade over the chicken and cook for about 30 minutes, turning at least once. Serve with noodles or rice.

35 minutes

★ ★

Serves 4

INGREDIENTS

1 lime

2.5cm (1in) piece fresh root ginger

1 clove garlic, crushed

2 tbsp oil

1 tbsp soy sauce

4 large chicken breasts

salt and ground black pepper

noodles or rice to serve

Minced Beef & Pasta Bake

INGREDIENTS

1 tbsp oil

450g (1lb) minced beef or lamb

1 large onion, chopped

1 clove garlic, crushed

1 x 400g (14oz) can chopped
tomatoes

1 tbsp tomato purée

1 tbsp Worcestershire sauce

1 tbsp finely chopped
flat-leaf parsley

170g (6oz) grated Cheddar cheese

230g (8oz) pasta, cooked until just
al dente

salt and ground black pepper

METHOD

1 Preheat the oven to 190°C (350°F) or Gas Mark 5. Heat the oil in a large oven proof dish, then cook the minced beef or lamb for about 10 minutes until browned.

2 Remove the meat from the pan and cook the onion and garlic, adding a little more oil if necessary. Return the meat to the pan, along with the tomatoes, tomato purée, Worcestershire sauce and chopped parsley.

3 Season well, then bring to the boil. Simmer for about 20 minutes. Stir in 110g (4oz) cheese and the pasta, then sprinkle the remaining cheese on top. Transfer to the oven and cook for 25–30 minutes until the dish is hot through and the cheese is bubbling.

 80 minutes

  ★ ★

Serves 4

Orange Chicken

METHOD

1 Preheat the oven to 190°C (375°F) or Gas Mark 5. Place the chicken in an ovenproof casserole dish and pour over enough orange juice to cover it, add the bay leaves. Cook for about 1½ hours.

2 About 20 minutes before the end of the cooking time, bring a large pan of salted water to the boil and cook the rice until tender and all the water has been absorbed.

3 Ensure that the chicken is cooked thoroughly. Remove from the casserole dish and place on a bed of rice. Spoon over any of the remaining sauce then season with salt and ground black pepper - the rice will soak this up and give a lovely flavour to the dish.

90 minutes

★ ★

Serves 6

INGREDIENTS

1½kg (3lb) oven-ready chicken

1 litre (1½ pints) orange juice

3 bay leaves

salt and ground black pepper

mixed long-grain and wild rice or long-grain rice to serve

Oriental Salmon Steaks

INGREDIENTS

4 salmon steaks

teriyaki marinade sauce for brushing

small piece of root ginger, peeled and sliced

2 spring onions, finely chopped

noodles to serve

METHOD

1 Brush each salmon steak generously with the teriyaki sauce. Peel and slice the ginger and spring onions. Place a few slices of ginger and the chopped spring onions on top of each of the salmon steaks.

2 Leave the steaks in a cool place for at least 30 minutes to marinate. Grill the steaks under a medium grill for about 5 minutes on each side or until cooked through.

3 When the fish is opaque, remove from the grill and serve immediately on a bed of egg noodles (readily available from the supermarket).

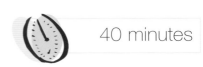 40 minutes

 ★

Serves 4

Pasta with Sausages

METHOD

1 Heat the oil in a large sauté pan. Slice the onions and fry for 10 minutes until golden brown. Chop the sausages into pieces, then add to the pan with the paprika. Fry, stirring continuously, for 2–3 minutes.

2 Add the stock, season and bring to the boil. Add the pasta, cover and simmer for about 15 minutes, or until the pasta is cooked. (Different types of pasta take varying times to cook, so check the instructions carefully.

3 Remove the pan from the heat and transfer to serving plates. Add a dollop of sour cream, then season to taste with salt and ground black pepper. Dust with paprika and serve.

35 minutes

★ ★

Serves 4

INGREDIENTS

2 tbsp oil

110g (4oz) onions, sliced

450g (1lb) meaty sausages, preferably spicy ones

2 tsp paprika

430ml (¾ pint) chicken stock

salt and ground black pepper

170g (6oz) pasta shapes, eg penne or fusilli or conchiglie

142ml (5fl oz) carton soured cream

paprika to garnish

Pasta with Tomato & Cream Cheese Sauce

INGREDIENTS

1 tbsp olive oil

1 large onion, sliced

1 clove garlic, crushed

1 x 400g (14oz) can
chopped tomatoes

1/2 tsp dried mixed herbs,
eg Herbes de Provence

salt and ground black pepper

340g (12oz) pasta shapes

1 x 100g (4oz) carton Philadelphia
cheese, or full-fat cream cheese

grated Parmesan and/or
fresh herbs to serve

METHOD

1 Heat the oil over a medium heat, add the onion and garlic and fry for about five minutes until soft but not browned. Lower the heat and add the chopped tomatoes and mixed herbs.

2 Season with salt and ground black pepper and cook for about 10 minutes. In the meantime, bring a large pan of salted water to the boil and cook the pasta, following the instructions on the packet.

3 Stir the Philadelphia cheese into the tomato sauce, making sure to remove any lumps, and heat through for 2-3 minutes. Pour the sauce over the cooked pasta and serve with Parmesan and/or fresh herbs.

 25 minutes

  ★ ★

Serves 4-6

Perfect Macaroni Cheese

METHOD

1 Cook the macaroni in large pan of boiling, salted water, according to the packet instructions. Meanwhile, melt the butter in a heavy-based pan, then add the flour. Stir for about 1 minute then gradually add the milk, stirring continuously.

2 When the sauce has thickened, add the grated cheese and nutmeg and stir continuously until the cheese has melted into the milk. Season with salt and ground black pepper. Mash the cooked broccoli and mix into the sauce.

3 When the macaroni is cooked, drain, then mix well with the sauce and broccoli. Sprinkle with extra grated cheese and place under a hot grill for a few minutes until the cheese is brown and bubbling.

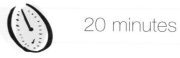

20 minutes

★ ★

Serves 6

INGREDIENTS

340g (12oz) macaroni

salt and ground black pepper

40g (1½oz) butter

30g (1oz) flour

300ml (½ pint) milk

110g (4oz) strong cheese, grated

pinch of nutmeg

170g (6oz) cooked broccoli

extra grated cheese for sprinkling

Perfect Mashed Potatoes

INGREDIENTS

680g (1½lb) potatoes

140ml (5fl oz) warm milk

85g (3oz) butter

salt and ground black pepper

SUGGESTIONS

110g (4oz) grated cheese

4 tbsp chopped mint – delicious with lamb

4 tbsp finely chopped flat-leafed parsley or dill – ideal for fish

METHOD

1 Peel the potatoes and cut into chunks. Bring a large pan of salted water to the boil, add the potatoes and cook for about 20 minutes or until tender. Be careful not to overcook the potatoes at this stage or they will retain too much of the water.

2 Drain well and return to the pan. Over a low heat, mash the potatoes using either a potato ricer or traditional masher (don't be tempted to use a food processor or you will end up with potato glue) then add the milk and butter.

3 Mix well and season to taste with salt and ground black pepper. Add the grated cheese or herbs as suggested and serve immediately.

30 minutes

★ ★

Serves 4

Pork Escalopes with Cheese

METHOD

1 Lightly brush the pork escalopes with oil, then sprinkle with the dried sage. Grill under a medium heat for about 10 minutes, or until half cooked, turning once.

2 Mix the grated cheese and cider, if using, thoroughly season with salt and ground black pepper, then sprinkle on top of the pork. Grill for a further 5-10 minutes or until the meat is cooked through.

3 When the cheese is brown and bubbling, remove from the grill and serve immediately with fresh seasonal vegetables. Try this dish with mashed potatoes and green beans or a crisp green salad.

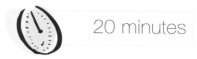 20 minutes

  ★

Serves 6

INGREDIENTS

6 pork escalopes

oil for brushing

1 tsp dried sage

170g (6oz) mature Cheddar cheese, grated

1 tbsp dry cider (optional)

salt and ground black pepper

Roast Vegetable Medley

INGREDIENTS

450g (1lb) sweet potatoes

450g (1lb) parsnips

230g (8oz) carrots

450g (1lb) squash, such as butternut

230g (8oz) courgettes

2 tsp caraway seeds

olive oil

2-3 cloves garlic, halved

salt and ground black pepper

warm crusty bread to serve

METHOD

1 Preheat the oven to 200°C (400°F) or Gas Mark 6. Peel the sweet potatoes, parsnips and carrots. Peel the squash and remove the seeds. Cut the peeled vegetables and the courgettes into roughly even bite-size chunks and place in a single layer in a roasting tin.

2 Stir the caraway seeds into the oil and then drizzle this over the vegetables. Scatter the garlic cloves over the dish, then season well with salt and ground black pepper. Make sure the vegetables are not too crowded, or they will steam instead of roasting.

3 Cook the vegetables in the preheated oven for about 30-40 minutes, shaking the tin from time to time to ensure that the vegetables are evenly browned. Serve with warmed crusty bread.

 1 hour

 ★ ★

Serves 6-8

BUDGET NOTE

Use the cheapest seasonal vegetables for this dish; any combination will do but they must be fresh!

Salmon Steaks with Crème Fraîche & Watercress

METHOD

1 Preheat the oven to 190°C (375°F) or Gas Mark 5. Brush each salmon steak with oil to prevent it sticking and arrange them individually on pieces of baking foil.

2 Top each salmon steak with a bay leaf and 1 tbsp of white wine, then season generously with salt and ground black pepper. Fold the foil up to make a parcel, leaving a space above the fish for steam to circulate.

3 Cook in the preheated oven for 15-20 minutes, or until the salmon is opaque. In the meantime, chop the watercress finely and stir it into the crème fraîche. Serve the sauce as an accompaniment to the salmon.

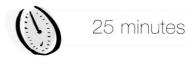 25 minutes

 ★ ★

Serves 4

INGREDIENTS

4 salmon steaks

oil for brushing

4 bay leaves

4 tbsp white wine

salt and ground black pepper

small bunch watercress

200g (7oz) carton crème fraîche

Spanish Omelette

INGREDIENTS

110ml (4fl oz) olive oil

340g (12oz) onions, thinly sliced

680g (1lb 8oz) potatoes, peeled
and thinly sliced

1 red pepper, sliced

6 eggs, beaten

salt and ground black pepper

chopped parsley to garnish

METHOD

1 Heat the oil in a large non-stick frying pan, add the sliced onions and pepper and cook gently for about 10 minutes or until soft. Add the potatoes, and cook for about 15 minutes until golden brown.

2 Using a slotted spoon, remove the vegetables from the pan, and then stir these into the beaten eggs, seasoning well with salt and ground black pepper. Heat the oil again, adding a little more if nescessary, then pour in the egg and potato mixture.

3 Cook over a medium heat for about 10 minutes or until well browned. Place under a hot grill for 2-3 minutes to brown the top, garnish with chopped parsley, then serve with a crisp green salad.

 45 minutes

 ★ ★

Serves 6

Spicy Chicken Pasta Sauce

METHOD

1 Heat the oil in a large pan, then add the chicken, browning it well. Remove the chicken from the pan, add the onion and garlic, plus a little more oil if necessary and cook for about 10 minutes until soft but not browned.

2 Return the chicken to the pan, stir in the cayenne pepper, ginger and chilli powder and cook for 2-3 minutes. Add the stock, stirring, then bring to the boil. Season with salt and ground black pepper. Cover and simmer for about 30 minutes.

3 Stir in 2 tbsp soured cream. Cook the pasta according to the instructions and arrange on serving plates. Place some sauce on top of the pasta, add an additional spoon of soured cream to each serving and sprinkle with cayenne pepper.

 1 hour

  ★ ★

Serves 6

INGREDIENTS

1 tbsp oil

340g (12oz) chicken breast, cut into chunks

1 large onion, chopped

1 clove garlic, crushed

1 tsp cayenne pepper, plus extra for sprinkling

½ tsp ground ginger

½ tsp chilli powder

300ml (½ pint) chicken stock

salt and ground black pepper

soured cream and cooked pasta to serve

Spicy Lamb with Potatoes

INGREDIENTS

oil

450g (1lb) minced lamb

1 large onion, cut into slices

1 clove garlic, crushed

1 x 400g (14oz) can
chopped tomatoes

1 tbsp cumin

1 tsp ground ginger

1 tbsp flat-leaf parsley, chopped

1 tbsp mint, chopped

300ml (½ pint) lamb stock

salt and ground black pepper

340g (12oz) small potatoes, cooked

1 x 400g (14oz) can
chickpeas

crusty bread to serve

METHOD

1 Heat 1 tbsp oil in a large, heavy-based pan. Add the minced lamb to the oil and cook until browned. Remove the lamb from the pan. Add the sliced onion and garlic, plus a little more oil if necessary and cook for about 10 minutes until soft, but not browned.

2 Return the lamb to the pan, add the can of chopped tomatoes, cumin, ground ginger, parsley and mint. Stir well, add the stock and season with salt and ground black pepper to taste.

3 Bring to the boil, then simmer for about 30 minutes. Add the potatoes and the drained chickpeas. Cook for a further 10 minutes until heated through. Serve with crusty bread.

 80 minutes

 ★ ★

Serves 6

Steak with Blue Cheese Butter

METHOD

1 Brush the steaks lightly with oil. Beat the softened butter, blue cheese and crushed garlic together and spoon on to each of the steaks.

2 Place under a preheated medium grill for 5-10 minutes depending on how you like your steak cooked. Season with salt and pepper to serve.

3 As the blue cheese brings out the flavour of the steak, it is best to team this dish with something simple like a green leaf salad or fresh vegetables.

 15 minutes

  ★

Serves 4

INGREDIENTS

4 x 175g (6oz) steaks, eg sirloin or rump

oil for brushing

55g (2oz) softened butter

55g (2oz) blue cheese, eg Stilton

1 clove garlic, crushed

salt and ground black pepper

Thai Vegetable Curry

INGREDIENTS

1 tbsp oil

1 large onion, chopped

1 clove garlic, crushed

170g (6oz) carrots, sliced on the diagonal

170g (6oz) small new potatoes

4 tbsp green curry paste

300ml (½ pint) coconut milk

300ml (½ pint) vegetable stock

1 stalk lemongrass

3 kaffir lime leaves

1 large red pepper, thinly sliced

110g (4oz) mangetout

110g (4oz) baby corn on the cob

noodles or rice to serve

METHOD

1 Heat the oil in a large pan or wok, then add the onion, garlic and carrots. Cook for about 10 minutes until soft, then add the potatoes, curry paste, coconut milk, stock, lemon grass and lime leaves.

2 Bring to the boil then simmer for about 20 minutes. Stir in the pepper, mangetout and baby corn and cook for a further 5-10 minutes until heated through but still retaining some crunch.

3 Meanwhile, in a large pan of boiling, salted water, cook the noodles or rice. You could use Thai rice, available from major supermarkets. Once all the vegetables are cooked, but still crunchy, remove from the pan and serve with either noodles or rice.

 50 minutes

  ★ ★

Serves 4

Tofu, Yellow Bean Sauce & Mangetout Stir-fry

METHOD

1 Heat the sunflower oil in a wok. When the oil is very hot, cook the sliced onion and carrots for about 5 minutes, stirring continuously until they begin to soften.

2 Add the tofu and yellow bean sauce to the wok, then cook for a further 10 minutes. Both these products are widely available from major supermarkets and ethnic food shops.

3 Stir in the mangetout and cook for about 2-3 minutes. Remove from the wok and serve with rice or noodles. Stir-fries like this one can also be served as a tasty filling for jacket potatoes.

 20 minutes

  ★

Serves 2

INGREDIENTS

1 tbsp sunflower oil

1 large onion, thinly sliced

110g (4oz) carrots, sliced on the diagonal

230g (8oz) firm tofu

½ jar yellow bean sauce
(available from supermarkets)

110g (4oz) mangetout

rice or noodles to serve

Traditional Fish Cakes

INGREDIENTS

340g (12oz) cod or haddock

150ml (¼ pint) milk

450g (1lb) potatoes, peeled and cut into chunks

salt and ground black pepper

30g (1oz) butter

4 spring onions, finely chopped

2 tbsp lemon juice

2 tbsp flat-leaf parsley, finely chopped

1 egg, beaten

55g (2oz) fresh white breadcrumbs

30g (1oz) plain flour

oil for frying

flat-leaf parsley for garnish

METHOD

1 Place the fish in a pan with just enough milk to cover it. Bring to the boil, lower the heat and poach for about 15 minutes, until the fish begins to flake. Meanwhile, cook the potatoes in boiling salted water until soft. Drain well, then mash.

2 Drain the fish, discarding any bones and skin. Mix the fish and the poaching milk with the mashed potatoes. Melt the butter in a pan, add the spring onions and cook for 5 minutes. Add to the fish mixture with the lemon juice, parsley and seasoning.

3 Add the beaten egg and some plain flour to the mixture to prevent it from falling apart and shape into balls. Dust with plain flour, coat in breadcrumbs and press firmly with the flat of your hand. Chill for 30 minutes. Heat the oil, then fry the fish cakes for 5 minutes on each side. Serve with tomato sauce.

1 hour

★ ★

Serves 4

Tuna Bake

METHOD

1 Preheat the oven to 200°C (400°F) or Gas Mark 6. Heat the oil, then cook the onion and garlic for 5-10 minutes until soft but not browned. Add the tomatoes, tuna, thyme and lemon juice, then season well with salt and ground black pepper.

2 Bring to the boil, then simmer over a low heat for 10-15 minutes, until the tomato sauce has thickened. In the meantime, cook and drain the pasta according to the packet instructions. Stir the pasta into the tomato and tuna mixture.

3 Stir in half the grated cheese and transfer the mixture to an ovenproof dish. Sprinkle the remainder of the cheese on top of the mixture and transfer to the oven. Cook for about 20 minutes until the cheese has melted and is brown and bubbling.

 50 minutes

  ★ ★

Serves 2

INGREDIENTS

1 tbsp olive oil

1 large onion, chopped

1 clove garlic, crushed

1 x 400g (14oz) can chopped tomatoes

1 x 400g (14oz) can tuna, drained

1 tbsp fresh chopped thyme or 1tsp dried

1 tbsp lemon juice

salt and ground black pepper

340g (12oz) pasta shapes

170g (6oz) Cheddar cheese, grated

Turkey with Sage & Grapes

INGREDIENTS

110g (4oz) streaky bacon

4 turkey or chicken breasts

about 8 fresh sage leaves or 1 tsp dried sage

salt and ground black pepper

olive oil

40g (1½oz) butter

55g (2oz) grapes

METHOD

1 Preheat the oven to 190°C (375°F) or Gas Mark 5. Wrap a piece of bacon around each turkey breast. Tie in place with string, tuck 2 sage leaves into the string and season well. If using dried sage, sprinkle it over the turkey.

2 In an ovenproof casserole, heat the oil and butter together. When hot, add the turkey breasts and cook until browned. Place in the oven and cook for 15 minutes.

3 Remove the turkey from the oven and add the grapes. Return to the oven and cook for a further 15 minutes until cooked through. Serve immediately.

 40 minutes

 ★

Serves 4

Vegetarian Noodles

M E T H O D

1 Heat the oil in a wok until very hot. Add the carrots, bamboo shoots, mangetout and pepper and cook for about 5 minutes or until the vegetables are beginning to soften but are still slightly crunchy to the bite.

2 Meanwhile, cook the noodles according to the instructions on the packet. Once the noodles and vegetables are cooked, as above, place the noodles in the wok with the vegetables.

3 Season with black pepper, then add the soy sauce, stir and remove from the heat. Serve sprinkled with sunflower seeds and garnished with flat-leaf parsley.

10 minutes

★ ★

Serves 4

I N G R E D I E N T S

1 tbsp sunflower oil

230g (8oz) carrots, cut into diagonal slices

1 x 230g (8oz) can bamboo shoots (available from supermarkets), drained

230g (8oz) mangetout or sugar-snap peas

1 red pepper, cut into thin strips

flat-leaf parsley to garnish

ground black pepper

1 tbsp soy sauce

1 tbsp sunflower seeds (optional)

340g (12oz) egg noodles

Puddings

Baked Bananas

INGREDIENTS

6 ripe bananas

85g (3oz) softened butter

110ml (4fl oz) dark rum

55g (2oz) demerara sugar

vanilla ice cream to serve

METHOD

1 Peel the bananas, then place each one on a piece of foil. Add a knob of butter, 2 tbsp rum and a sprinkling of demerara sugar to each banana.

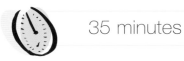 35 minutes

 ★

2 Wrap the foil quite tightly around the banana to make a parcel. Preheat the oven to 180°C (350°F) or Gas Mark 4. You could also cook these on a barbecue if you're eating al fresco.

Serves 6

3 Cook for approximately 30 minutes or until the banana is soft and serve with vanilla ice cream or whipped cream. To continue the Caribbean theme, accompany this pudding with a small glass of rum.

Boozy Bread & Butter Pudding

METHOD

1 Soak the sultanas in brandy overnight until they plump up. Preheat the oven to 180°C (350°F) or Gas Mark 4. Grease a 1 litre (2 pint) baking dish with butter.

2 Butter the slices of bread and then cut in half. Arrange half of these in the base of the baking dish. Cover with half of the sultanas, then layer the remaining bread on top, and finish with the remaining sultanas.

3 Stir the sugar into the milk, then add the beaten eggs. Pour this mixture over the bread, dust with nutmeg and bake for 35–45 minutes. Serve warm with vanilla ice cream or double cream dusted with nutmeg.

1 hour

★ ★

Serves 4

INGREDIENTS

85g (3oz) sultanas

60ml (2fl oz) brandy

butter for greasing

8 small slices bread, buttered

85g (3oz) caster sugar

300ml (½ pint) milk

3 eggs

ground nutmeg

Chocolate Sensation

INGREDIENTS

230g (8oz) dark chocolate

5 eggs, separated

110g (4oz) softened unsalted butter

110g (4oz) caster sugar

230g (8oz) sponge fingers

1 cup strong black coffee

whipped cream to serve

sprig of mint to decorate

METHOD

1 Melt the chocolate in a small bowl over a saucepan of simmering water, making sure that the bowl doesn't come into contact with the water or the chocolate will burn. Allow to cool slightly, then add the egg yolks, butter and sugar.

2 Whip the egg whites until stiff, then add to the chocolate mixture. Next, line the base of a loose bottomed cake tin with greaseproof paper. Dip the sponge fingers lightly into the coffee and line the inside of the tin. Ensure that when standing, the fingers are closely packed (see photo).

3 Fill the middle of the tin with the chocolate mixture and chill for at least 24 hours. Remove gently from the tin, by pushing up the bottom, and top with whipped cream.

 25 minutes

 ★ ★ ★

Serves 6

Classic Chocolate Mousse

M E T H O D

1 Melt the chocolate, without stirring, in a small bowl over a pan of simmering water, making sure that the bowl does not come into contact with the water or the chocolate will burn. Pour in the rum or brandy.

2 Beat the egg yolks and add them to the hot chocolate, beating well. Leave to stand for about 10 minutes. In the meantime, beat the egg whites until they form soft peaks, then stir in to the cooled chocolate mixture.

3 Transfer to the serving dishes or glasses and chill for 2-3 hours until firm. Just before serving, dust each one with a grating of white chocolate (keep this in the fridge so it is really hard and easier to grate) and a dusting of cocoa powder.

25 minutes

★ ★ ★

Serves 4

I N G R E D I E N T S

230g (8oz) good-quality dark chocolate

4 eggs, separated

2-3 tbsp dark rum or brandy

grated white chocolate and cocoa powder to serve

Dried Fruit Compôte with Greek Yogurt

INGREDIENTS

300ml (½ pint) unsweetened
orange or apple juice

30g (1oz) demerara sugar

55g (2oz) raisins

110g (4oz) no-soak dried apricots

55g (2oz) dried figs (optional)

1 cinnamon stick

1 apple

1 pear

1 large orange

1 x 200g (7oz) carton Greek
yogurt or fromage frais to serve

METHOD

1 Place the orange juice, sugar, raisins, apricots, figs and cinnamon stick in a large pan. Heat, stirring to dissolve the sugar, for about 10 minutes or until the apricots are tender.

2 Peel, core and slice the apple and pear, then immediately add to the compôte mixture, or they will turn brown. Cook for a further 5 minutes or until all the fruit is tender.

3 Remove from the heat, then add the orange, cut into segments. Leave to cool, then serve with spoonfuls of Greek yogurt or fromage frais.

 15 minutes

 ★

Serves 4

Fruit Salad on a Budget

METHOD

1 Heat 140ml (5fl oz) water and add the sugar to make a syrup; if you are feeling extravagant, add a few tbsp brandy or whisky for extra flavour!

2 Remove all pips, seeds, cores, and skin and chop the fruit into bite-size chunks. Place in a bowl and pour the syrup over the fruit.

3 Leave the fruit to soak up the syrup for at least 3 hours, but ensure that the apples, bananas and pears are added at the last minute or they will go brown.

 25 minutes

  ★

Serves 4

BUDGET NOTE

Concentrate on cheaper fruits for this recipe, adding just one or two of the more expensive – such as strawberries – for colour and flavour.

INGREDIENTS

Use any combination of the following fruits, choosing ones that are ripe and in season
(see chart on pages 8–9): apples, starfruit, banana, oranges, grapefruit, strawberries, grapes, pears, pineapple, mangoes, guava, papaya, kiwi fruit

30g (1oz) sugar

brandy or whisky (optional)

Norwegian Apple Cake

INGREDIENTS

170g (6oz) softened butter

170g (6oz) caster sugar

3 large eggs, beaten

170g (6oz) self-raising flour, sieved

2 cooking apples, peeled cored and thinly sliced

ground cinnamon

200g (7oz) carton fresh custard (available from supermarkets)

55g (2oz) flaked almonds

whipped cream to serve

METHOD

1 In a mixing bowl, cream the butter and sugar together until light and fluffy. Next beat the eggs together and gradually add to the creamed butter. Gently fold in the flour using a metal spoon.

2 Put the mixture in a greased tin and spread evenly with a pallette knife. Arrange the apple slices on top of the mixture. Sprinkle with cinnamon and pour over the fresh custard.

3 Cook at 200°C (400°F) or Gas Mark 6 for about 30 minutes, or until the middle is set and the edges are brown. To serve, sprinkle with flaked almonds and/or top with whipped cream dusted with cinnamon.

 45 minutes

 ★ ★ ★

Serves 8

Queen of Puddings

METHOD

1 Preheat the oven to 180°C (350°F) or Gas Mark 4. Bring the milk to the boil in a small saucepan. Remove from the heat and add the breadcrumbs, butter, 30g (1 oz) sugar and the lemon rind. Leave to stand for 20–30 minutes.

2 Add the egg yolks to the cooled mixture, pour into a greased 900ml (1½ pint) pie dish and cook for about 35 minutes. Meanwhile, melt the jam over a low heat and spread it over the cooked egg and breadcrumb mixture.

3 Beat the egg whites until stiff, then whisk in 30g (1oz) caster sugar. Spoon this meringue on top of the jam. Sprinkle 1 tsp caster sugar on top and cook in the oven for a further 10–15 minutes or until golden brown.

 70 minutes

  ★ ★

Serves 4

INGREDIENTS

600ml (1 pint) milk

110g (4oz) fresh white breadcrumbs

15g (½oz) butter

55g (2oz) caster sugar

grated rind of 1 lemon

2 eggs, separated

3 tbsp blackcurrant or raspberry jam

Raspberry Sensation

INGREDIENTS

85g (3oz) porridge oats

230g (8oz) fresh or 300g (11oz) can raspberries (see Budget Note)

1 x 200g (7oz) carton Greek yogurt

4 tbsp demerara sugar

METHOD

1 Toast the oats until golden brown – be careful as they burn easily – then set aside to cool. If using fresh raspberries, reserve 2 then mash them lightly with a fork; if using canned, drain them thoroughly.

2 Gently stir the raspberries and oats into the Greek yogurt, then transfer the mixture into individual heatproof bowls or glasses.

3 Sprinkle the demerara sugar over the top, then flash under a hot grill for 2-3 minutes until the sugar has caramelised. Serve immediately.

 10 minutes

  ★

Serves 2

BUDGET NOTE

Fresh raspberries can be expensive, even when in season. If you prefer, you can try this recipe with blackcurrants, blueberries or even very ripe strawberries.

Rice Pudding with Dried Fruits

METHOD

1 Preheat the oven to 150°C (300°F) or Gas Mark 2. Place the rice in a saucepan, add the milk and bring slowly to the boil. Simmer for about 10 minutes.

2 Add the sugar and butter and stir well until melted, then remove the mixture from the heat. When cool, add the beaten eggs, sultanas and apricots.

3 Pour into a well buttered 1 litre (2 pint) baking dish, then sprinkle over the ground nutmeg. Cook for 30–40 minutes. For a touch of decadence, serve with a splash of cream.

1 hour

★ ★

Serves 4

INGREDIENTS

110g (4oz) pudding rice

900ml (1½ pints) milk

85g (3oz) caster sugar

55g (2oz) butter

3 eggs

110g (4oz) sultanas

55g (2oz) dried apricots,
cut into pieces

ground nutmeg

Apricot & Orange Smoothie

INGREDIENTS

170g (6oz) fresh apricots, or a
small can in juice

300ml (½ pint) orange juice

1 tsp honey

pinch of cinnamon

140g (5oz) carton natural yogurt

METHOD

1 Smoothies can be made using virtually any fruit, or even combinations of fruit (see alternative recipes).

2 Simply combine all of the ingredients in a blender until smooth. Pour into separate glasses. Allow to chill for 10-15 minutes if possible.

3 If serving to guests, decorate each glass with a slice of fresh fruit or a twist of peel.

 5 minutes

 ★

Serves 2

These drinks are popular in America and Australia as they are nutritional and healthy and make perfect high-speed breakfasts!

Banana & Orange Smoothie

M E T H O D

1 Chop the banana into even-sized pieces, then place in a blender with the orange juice and natural yogurt.

2 Whizz for a few seconds, then add the ice cubes or crushed ice. Process again until all the ingredients are combined.

3 Serve the smoothie in tall glasses with a thin sliver, or twist, of orange peel. Drink immediately or the banana will turn the smoothie an unappetising brown colour.

 5 minutes

 ★

Serves 2

I N G R E D I E N T S

2 large ripe bananas

300ml (½ pint) orange juice

140g (5oz) carton natural yogurt

a handful of ice cubes

Apple & Pear Smoothie

INGREDIENTS

2 ripe eating apples

2 ripe pears

300ml (½ pint) apple juice

150g (5oz) carton natural yogurt

Alternative recipes

For an even easier recipe, try a fresh banana milkshake with 1 banana, 600 ml (1 pint) of cold milk. Break the banana into chunks, add to milk and blend!

METHOD

1 Peel, core and slice the fruit. Keep aside two slices each of apple and pear for decoration, then cook the rest over a medium heat in half of the apple juice for 10–15 minutes until the fruit is soft.

2 When cooked, allow to cool. Transfer the fruit to the blender with the remaining apple juice and the natural yogurt.

3 Blend until smooth and serve immediately, with a slice of fruit added to the side of the glass for decoration. Do not be tempted to make this smoothie in advance as the apple will turn it an unappetising brown colour.

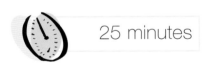 25 minutes

 ★ ★

Serves 2

Steamed Syrup Pudding

METHOD

1 Beat the margarine and sugar in a bowl until creamy. Gradually add the eggs, then fold in the sieved flour and ginger – you can do all this in the mixer if you prefer.

2 Grease a 600ml (1 pint) pudding basin with margarine. Cover the base with the golden syrup then carefully add the sponge mixture.

3 Tie greaseproof paper on top as a lid and steam in a large pan for 2 hours (you can place it in a colander over simmering water), topping up the water as and when necessary. Serve with warmed golden syrup and, if you are feeling really indulgent, clotted cream.

 2¼ hours

  ★ ★

Serves 4–6

INGREDIENTS

110g (4oz) sunflower margarine, plus extra for greasing

110g (4oz) dark brown (muscovado) sugar

2 eggs, beaten

170g (6oz) self-raising flour

½ tsp ground ginger

2-3 tbsp golden syrup

golden syrup and clotted cream to serve (optional)

Strawberries Dipped in Chocolate

INGREDIENTS

230g (8oz) good-quality dark chocolate, with minimum 60% cocoa solids

340g (12oz) strawberries

vanilla ice cream or single cream to serve

METHOD

1 Break the chocolate up and place in a small bowl over a pan of simmering water. The bowl must not touch the water as this will burn the chocolate, and you must ensure that no water gets into the chocolate.

2 Stir the chocolate from time to time until melted completely. Wash and pat dry the strawberries. Remove the chocolate from the heat and dip each strawberry in turn into the chocolate, holding by the stalk.

3 Ensure that the strawberry has an even coating of chocolate then place on a tray to cool. Chill in the fridge until the chocolate has hardened and then serve either with vanilla ice cream or single cream. This recipe also works well as a sweet item for a finger buffet.

20 minutes

 ★ ★

Serves 4

Zabaglione

METHOD

1 Whisk the egg yolks and sugar in a heatproof bowl until pale and creamy. Gradually whisk in the Marsala or sweet sherry until thoroughly combined.

2 Place the bowl over a barely simmering pan of water on a low heat until the mixture thickens. You'll have to be patient as this should take about 10 minutes.

3 As soon as the mixture thickens, transfer to individual serving bowls or glasses to serve. Finally, sprinkle grated chocolate over the top and enjoy!

 25 minutes

  ★ ★ ★

Serves 4

INGREDIENTS

8 egg yolks

3 tbsp caster sugar

85ml (3fl oz) Marsala or sweet sherry

110g (4oz) grated dark chocolate (optional)

Menu

Cheap and Cheerful

**PAGE 29
Chicken
Liver Paté**

**PAGE 18
Bean &
Lentil Salad**

**PAGE 85
Queen of
Puddings**

Serves 4

Dinner Party

**PAGE 13
Minted Pea &
Lettuce Soup**

**PAGE 65
Salmon Steaks
with Crème
Fraîche &
Watercress**

**PAGE 81
Classic
Chocolate
Mousse**

Serves 4

Lunch Party for friends

**PAGE 33
Pitta Pockets
with Tuna**

**PAGE 57
Orange
Chicken**

**PAGE 78
Baked
Bananas**

Serves 6

1
2
3

You can, of course, combine dishes to make some impressive menus without spending a fortune. Here are some ideas:

Vegetarian Party Menu

**PAGE 12
Chickpea
Soup**

**PAGE 66
Spanish
Omelette**

**PAGE 82
Dried Fruit
Compôte with
Greek Yogurt**

Serves 4

Quick and Easy Feast

**PAGE 15
Three-Bean
Soup**

**PAGE 74
Turkey with
Sage & Grapes**

**PAGE 83
Fruit Salad
on a Budget**

Serves 4

Indulgent Dinner

**PAGE 26
Thai-Style
Seafood Salad**

**PAGE 69
Steak with
Blue Cheese
Butter**

**PAGE 92
Strawberries
dipped in
Chocolate**

Serves 4

suggestions

Conversions

28g=1oz, and 28.5ml=1fl oz, but I have rounded up or down as follows:

METRIC IMPERIAL
30g = 1oz
55g = 2oz
85g = 3oz
110g = 4oz
140g = 5oz
170g = 6oz
200g = 7oz
230g = 8oz
340g = 12oz
450g = 1lb
1kg = 2lb 2oz

1 litre = 35fl oz (1 pint = 20fl oz)
30ml = 1 fl oz
60ml = 2fl oz
85ml = 3fl oz
110ml = 4fl oz
140ml = 5fl oz
600ml = 1 pint
300ml = ½ pint

ABBREVIATIONS
tbsp = tablespoon (15ml)
tsp = teaspoon (5ml)